The Ultimate Vegan Weed Cookbook: Marijuana Recipes for Vegans

By: B. Smooth Puffington

Contents:

Petruchio's Vegan Fudge
Pedant's Pecan Pie
Marcellus' Mango Cheesecake
King Lear's Loko Cake!
Brutus' Thunder Balls!
Cassio's Stuffed Jalapeños
Oswald's Chocolate Chip Cookies
Silvius Space Cookies

Advice from a poorly drawn cop...

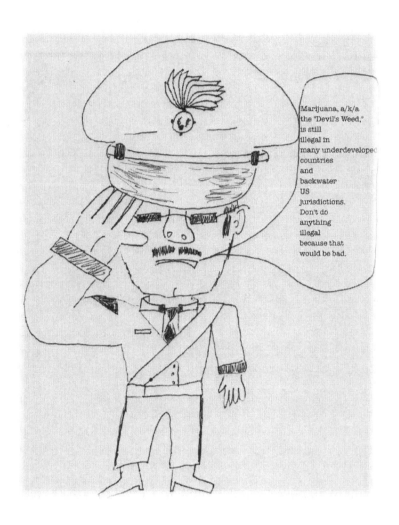

Cannabis Coconut Oil/Butter

Advisory: this recipe must be monitored for at least 12 hours.

Here's what you'll need:

A nice slow cooker/crockpot!
1 pound (450g) of Coconut Oil
A Very Fine, Metal Strainer
Cheesecloth
Meat Thermometer (Finally useful for something!)
1-3oz (28-35g) of dried marijuana, the more you add the bigger the buzz!

And here we go!

1. If you'd like, you can soak the weed in water overnight, then dry it before grinding. This reduces the marijuana flavor but won't lessen the THC count. Some people dislike the flavor, and others love it, so this step is optional according to personal taste.

2. Alright, so first let's grind that weed up nice and fine. If you have a coffee grinder, that would be perfect for this part. Just don't make it too powdery or it might be hard to strain out later.

3. Pop that coconut oil in the slow cooker, then pour in enough water so that the coconut oil floats on top. Crack that slow cooker to HIGH and let the oil melt into a liquid.

4. Stir your weed in slowly, until it's all in there and nice and wet. Add more water if you need to.

5. Pop that meat thermometer in the slow cooker so you can monitor the temperature. Once it looks like it's close to 250° F (120° C), dial her back to LOW and stir.

6. Stir every now and then, always monitoring the temperature to make sure it's in around 250° F (120° C) and never exceeds 270° F (135° C). You may need to toggle the dial between LOW and HIGH to achieve this temperature.

7. Keep adding water through this process to make sure the weed stays submerged. This helps prevent the THC from burning off.

8. After 12-18 hours of this, turn off your slow cooker and let it cool a bit.

9. Take that cheesecloth and line your strainer with it. Place the strainer over a large cooking pot to catch the liquid that comes out the bottom.

10. Pour the liquid from the slow cooker into the strainer, nice and easy, a little at a time.

11. If the liquid isn't too hot, squeeze that cheesecloth like a teabag to get all that precious THC oil out of it.

12. You can discard the pulp inside the cheesecloth and place that cooking pot into the fridge overnight to cool.

13. The next morning you'll see that the oil will be a solid floating on top of the water, from which it separated as it was cooling.

14. You can wrap that oil in plastic wrap or place it in any container and store it in the fridge from when you need it. The oil is good to use in place of butter in many recipes and you can even pop some of it in tea, coffee and hot cocoa!

Cannabis Almond Milk

Here's what you'll need:

½ Cup of Raw Almonds
3 Cups of distilled water
1-4 grams of coarsely ground cannabis
Cheesecloth
Food Processor

And here we go!

1. Soak those almonds overnight, drain and rinse them the next morning!

2. Blend those almonds along with the water in your food processor!

3. Strain that almond milk through the cheesecloth, and into a pot, you can throw out or eat the little almond bits that get left behind.

4.   Bring that almond milk up to a light boil over low heat.

5.   Pop in the cannabis and let her simmer for two hours, stirring frequently

6.   Let the brew cool down completely, then strain through the cheesecloth again, collecting that sweet, sweet liquid in a container below. Store in the fridge for up to two weeks!

Cannabis Olive Oil or Vegetable Oil

Here's what you'll need:

1 oz (28g) of finely ground buds, or 2 oz (56g) of dried, and well-ground, trimmed leaf
6 cups of olive oil or vegetable oil

And here we go!

1. Get that oil in a saucepan and heat it up slowly. Once you get a whiff of the oil's aroma, add a little ground weed. Keep adding weed, little by little, until it's all in there and covered with oil.

2. Simmer that brew on low heat for 45 minutes, stirring every now and then.

3. Take the saucepan off the stove and let it all cool down.

4. Take a metal strainer and lined it with cheesecloth, pour the oil/weed mixture through the strainer/cheesecloth over a nice big container, then wring out the cheesecloth like a teabag to make sure you get all that nice THC oil out of it.

5. You can then store the oil in an airtight container for up to two months in the fridge. This oil is good to use for any oily application, just remember that high temps will burn off the THC.

———————————————————————————

Hemp Seed Pesto

Here's what you'll need:

1 cup of fresh, chopped basil leaves
3 cloves of garlic
1/2 cup of kale leaves chopped up with the rib removed
1 tablespoon of yeast
1/4 cup of lightly toasted hemp seeds
2 tablespoons of hempseed oil
1/4 cup of Cannabis Olive Oil
1 tablespoon of lemon juice
½ teaspoon of fresh ground black pepper
½ teaspoon of course salt

And here we go!

1. Boil yourself up a small pot of water. Alongside it, get bowl and put some ice cubes and cold water in it.

2. Blanch the basil and kale in the pot for 30 seconds, then pop it in the ice water. Then shake it dry and put it in a food processor.

3. Take the garlic, salt, pepper natural yeast, lemon juice and hemp seeds, and pop that all in the food processor as well.

4. Pulse that puppy until everything is nice and even and shredded, then add the Cannabis Olive Oil and hempseed oil, then give it one more good pulse to mix everything together.

5. You can use this immediately or put it in a container in the fridge for later use. It should hold up to two weeks!

Iago's Mushroom Soup

Here's what you'll need:

1 tablespoon of olive oil
2 tablespoon of earth balance butter
4 tablespoons Cannabis Olive Oil
1 tablespoon of toasted sesame oil
1 pound (450g) of portobello mushrooms, sliced
1 medium carrot, peeled and diced
1 pound (450g) of sliced cremini mushrooms, sliced
3 tablespoons of finely chopped green onions
1 cup of pearl onions, thawed of packaged frozen
3 cloves of garlic, minced
1 small onion, julienned
2 teaspoons of fresh thyme leaves, lightly chopped
2 tablespoons of organic tomato paste
1 1/2 cup of full-bodied red wine (organic!)
1 ½ tablespoons of white, whole-wheat flour
2 ¼ cups of organic vegetable broth
1 ½ tablespoons of nutritional yeast
2 cups of cooked quinoa, farro, or noodles
Sea and pepper, to taste

1 tablespoon toasted sesame seeds

And here we go!

1. Get that tablespoon of regular olive oil and heat her up together with one tablespoon of earth balance in a heavy pan over medium heat.

2. Sauté the julienned onions with some salt and pepper until they turn brown and translucent. This should take about 15 minutes. Once they're cooked, take the julienned onions out of the pan and set them aside.

3. Swish ¼ of the vegetable broth and some Cannabis Olive oil around in the pan, then sear up the pearl onions and mushrooms, a little bit at a time. Set them aside once they're cooked.

4. Now set the flame to low and add 2 tablespoons of the Cannabis Olive Oil along with thyme, green onions, and carrots. Toss in a pinch of salt and pepper and cook that up for 10 minutes or so, stirring now and again. Now add in your garlic and let that go for another 2 minutes.

5. Add some red wine and swish it around in the pot, scraping at any bits of food that might be stuck to the bottom. Turn the heat up to medium and reduce the wine until you have about half what you started with, then add the tomato paste and the rest of the broth. Also pop those fried onions and mushrooms in there while you're at it.

6. Let the pot return to a boil then bring it down to a simmer, adding the yeast and any Cannabis Olive Oil that might be left. Simmer that bad boy for 15 minutes.

7. After 15, minutes, toss the remaining ingredients (except the noodles/faro/quinoa) into the pot and let it blend in there.

8. Now you have a nice, tasty sauce to pour over your carb of choice! You can sprinkle sesame seeds or add a dollop of sour cream if you'd like!

Prospero's Pumpkin Spice Pancakes

Here's what you'll need:
1 cup of vanilla soymilk
2 tablespoons of agave nectar
1 tablespoon of lemon juice
1/4 cup of Cannabis Coconut Oil
1 cup of white whole-wheat flour
3 ripe bananas
1 teaspoon of vanilla extract
1/2 cup of all purpose flour
1 teaspoon of pumpkin pie spice
1 teaspoon of baking powder
1 teaspoon of baking soda
1/2 cup of walnut pieces, for sprinkling in while cooking
¼ teaspoon of cinnamon
½ teaspoon of salt
½ tablespoon of earth balance butter

And here we go!

1. Combine that soymilk and lemon juice in a small bowl and whisk it together, then let it sit for 5 minutes.

2. In a medium bowl, mix the flours, salt, spices, baking powder, and baking soda, then set it aside.

3. Take a large bowl and mash up those bananas in it! Add the agave nectar, soymilk/lemon juice mix, vanilla extract, and Cannabis Olive Oil.

4. Mix the dry ingredients in with the wet, little by little, whisking to get yourself a nice batter.

5. Get a large pan and put her on the stove over medium heat. Add some earth balance to the pan and make a little test pancake. If it comes out ok, continue on with the rest.

6. Make yo' pancakes!

7. Add some maple syrup.

8. Get buzzed for breakfast!

Beatrice's Blueberry and Banana Smoothie

Here's what you'll need:

1/2 cup of ice
2 tablespoons of honey
1 large, sliced banana
3/4 cup of Cannabis Almond Milk
8 fresh, sliced strawberries
1/2 cup of fresh blueberries

And here we go!

1. Pop it all in a blender.

2. Blend

3. Pour

4. Drink

5. Buzz

_____

Richard III's Guacamole Tacos!

Here's what you'll need:

Salsa:

2 limes squeezed for juice
1 cup of jicama, sliced in ¼ inch strips
1/4 cup of sliced radish
2 teaspoons of chopped cilantro
salt and pepper to taste

Beans:

¼ teaspoon of cayenne pepper
2 tablespoons of Cannabis Coconut Oil
1 can of vegan refried beans
1 teaspoon of cumin
black pepper to taste

Guac:

4 ripe avocados
2 cloves of garlic, minced
1/2 cup of diced tomatoes
2 tablespoons of Cannabis Coconut Oil

salt and pepper to taste
2 limes squeezed for juice
4 corn tortillas

And here we go!

1. Get that salsa together foo! Mix the jicama, radish, lime juice, and cilantro together in a small bowl. Set aside for now!

2. Get them beans cookin'! Heat that Cannabis Olive oil in a pan over medium heat. Add in your refried beans and stir in the rest, let her cook up for at least five minutes.

3. Guacamole time! Peel and split your avocados, then chop them up and pop the bits into a bowl, getting rid of the skin and pit. Add the rest of the ingredients and mash that baby together.

4. WELCOME TO TACOLAND! Heat up those tortillas and load them up as you see fit!

Osrick's Vegan Weed Brownies

Yield 8 Brownies

Here's what you'll need:

2 grams (1/8th ounce) of Weed
2 cups of brown sugar
200ml of olive oil
1 teaspoon of baking powder
2 cups of flour
1 teaspoon of salt
1 cup of water
1/2 cup of vegan chocolate chips
1/2 cup of cocoa powder
1 teaspoon of vanilla extract

And here we go!

1. Alright, so let's pre-heat that oven to 375 °F (180° C), and grind up the weed.

2. Next, let's heat some oil in a saucepan over a low flame, then toss in our weed. Let the weed simmer for 30 minutes, being careful to keep the temperature as low as possible. After 30 minutes take the pan off the flame and let it cool down completely.

3. In a large mixing bowl, stir together the dry ingredients. Then take a sieve and place it over the mixing bowl. Pour in your weed/oil mixture, pressing the weed with a spoon to wring out all that delicious THC oil.

4. Add the remaining ingredients to the mixing bowl and mix her up good.

5. Press the mixture onto greased or parchment lined baking sheet and pop her in the oven for half an hour.

6. It should take an hour or two after eating to arrive in paradise!

Jacque's Thai Soup

Here's what you'll need:
1 stalk of fresh, peeled and sliced, lemongrass
7 tablespoons of Cannabis Olive Oil
2 cans of coconut cream
1 small can of sliced water chestnuts, drain that puppy!
1/2 cup of mango juice
1 can sweet baby corn, drain that sucker and chop the corn up fine!
1/2 cup of chopped, green onion tops
3 tablespoons of chopped, fresh cilantro
1 ½ tablespoons of chopped, fresh mint
2 tablespoons of chopped, fresh basil
½ teaspoon of powdered ginger
2 tablespoons of curry powder
Half of a lime, squeezed for juice
1 teaspoon of sesame oil
1 tablespoon of delicious Sriracha hot sauce
Salt to taste

And here we go!

1. Got a heavy pot and place it on the stove over low heat.

2. Add the lemongrass and mango juice little by little, and bring it up to a simmer.

3. Toss in everything else, except the Cannabis Olive Oil, lime juice and sesame oil, and let it continue to simmer for another 15 minutes.

4. After 15 minutes, remove from heat. Add in the Cannabis Olive Oil, lime juice and sesame oil before serving.

5. Serve her up!

6. Get buzzed!

Horatio's Banana Ice Cream

Here's what you'll need:

2 cups of Cannabis Almond Milk
1 cup of Coconut Milk
1/2 cup of sugar
A pinch of salt
4 pureed bananas
1 tablespoon of corn starch
1/2 cup of peanut butter (you can remove this if you have allergies)

And here we go!

1. Grab that sugar, coconut milk, Cannabis Almond Milk, and cornstarch and pop it all in a large saucepan. Mix it all together right there in the pan.

2. Cover up the pan and place it on the stove over medium heat for about 10 minutes, until it thickens up a bit. Once it's a little thickened, take it off the stove and let it cool.

3. Once it's cooled down, place it in a large bowl and let it chill in the fridge for an hour. After an hour, stir it up and place some plastic wrap on top, then let it sit in the fridge for 24 hours.

4. After 24 hours, place the mixture in an airtight container and move it to the freezer, then wait 2 hours.

5. After 2 hours, stir in the banana puree and peanut butter and stir it up nice, then pop it back in the freezer for another 6 hours.

6. After 6 hours, your ice cream is ready to eat!

Calpurnia's Corn Salad

Here's what you'll need:

1/2 cup of Cannabis Olive Oil
6 ears of fresh, shucked and rinsed corn
1 red onion, chop 'er up!
1 can of black beans, drain that puppy!
1 red bell pepper, dice that puppy!
1 green bell pepper, dice that puppy!
4 minced cloves of garlic
1 cup of fresh, chopped cilantro
2 tablespoons of chipotle hot sauce
Juice from 3 limes

And here we go!

1. Get that grill going on high heat!

2. Grill up yo' corn! Set it aside to cool once it's cooked.

3. Cut away the delicious corn kernels and pop them in a mixing bowl.

4. Put everything else in a food processor and process that stuff!

5. Pour over corn.

6. Eat!

7. Get high!

_____

Mercutio's No-Bake Cookies

Here's what you'll need:
1/4 cup of natural crunchy peanut butter
1/4 cup of unsweetened, dutch-processed cocoa powder
1/2 cup of crunchy cookie butter
1/4 cup (60ml) cane sugar
1 ½ cups of vanilla soy milk
3 cups of quick cooking oats
1/4 cup of Cannabis Coconut Oil
2 teaspoons of vanilla extract
1/4 cup of earth balance butter
A pinch salt

And here we go!

1. Alright, get yourself a saucepan and pop her on the stove over medium heat. Now add the Cannabis Olive Oil, milk, earth balance, cocoa powder, and sugar. Stir it all up and bring it to a boil for a minute.

2. Decrease the heat a little and add the peanut butter and cookie butter, stir it in nice and good.

3. Remove from heat and add the vanilla, oats, and salt, stirring them right in.

4. Use a spoon to plop down some dollops on wax paper. Let them cool off for an hour and you're ready to go!

_____

Viola's Pesto Toast

Here's what you'll need:

1 slice of hearty whole-grain bread
2 tablespoon of Hemp Seed Pesto
1/4 cup of vegan mayo
2 teaspoons of Hempseeds

And here we go!

1. Get that hemp seed pesto from earlier and mix it together with some vegan mayo.

2. Spread that delicious creamy goodness on your favorite whole-grain toast!

Falstaff's Biscuits and Gravy

Yield 8

Here's what you'll need:

Biscuits:
1 cup of white whole-wheat flour
½ teaspoon of baking soda
1 cup of unbleached all-purpose flour
1 tablespoon of baking powder
¾ teaspoon of sea salt
1/4 cup of Cannabis Coconut Oil
¾ cup of unsweetened almond milk
1 tablespoon of lemon juice
5 tablespoon of earth balance butter

White Country-Style Gravy:
2 cups of unsweetened rice milk
1 ½ tablespoon of Cannabis Coconut Oil
sea salt and black pepper to taste
¼ cup of unbleached all-purpose flour
Rubbed sage to taste

And here we go!

Biscuits:

1. Get that oven pre-heated to 450°F (230°C)

2. In a small bowl, mix together the milk and lemon juice, then let it sit for 5 minutes. After 5 minutes, add the coconut cannabis oil and whisk it all together. Now, let that small bowl be for a little bit, we'll come back to it.

3. Get those dry ingredients in a large bowl and whisk them all together until combined.

4. Time for some fun! Chop up the butter and use your hands to fold it into the dry ingredients. If you're feeling more traditional, you could also use a pastry cutter instead of your hands. You want the whole mixture to get moist and granular.

5. Now add the milk to that dry mix, little by little, until you've worked it into a dough. Spread some flour on a cool, dry surface and knead the dough four or five times. Be careful not to knead it too much.

6. Tamp the dough out into a nice 1-inch thick (2.5cm) circle and use a jar lid or cookie cutter to cut biscuits out of it. Place the biscuits on a baking sheet, close enough to each other that they touch.

7. Brush the biscuits with some melted butter and sprinkle some salt over them. Bake those bad boys for 10-15 minutes. You want them to be just slightly browned on top.

8. Once they're out of the oven, you want to let them cool for a bit before eating them.

Gravy:

1. Melt down that cannabis coconut oil in a saucepan over low heat.

2. Whisk in the rest of the ingredients, adding the flour little by little.

3. Let that puppy simmer for a few minutes until it starts to thicken.

4. Once she's all combined, even and has thickened a little, take the saucepan off the stove and let her cool down a bit. You can now pour the gravy over your biscuits for an out of this world experience!

Julius Caesar's Chik'n Salad

Here's what you'll need:
1/2 cup of water
1 chick'n breast or similar brand, cook 'er up according to
directions, cut then chop her into tiny pieces
¾ cup of thin celery slices
2 cups of chickpeas, drained and rinse them well
1 tablespoon of Dijon mustard
1/2 cup of walnut pieces
2 tablespoon of Cannabis Coconut Oil
1/2 cup of vegan mayo
¼ teaspoon of black pepper
A pinch of salt
1/8 teaspoon of ground mustard seed
1 tablespoon of chopped, fresh dill

And here we go!

1. Let's get those chickpeas ready. Microwave them for two minutes, drain those bad boys, then mash them up. Leave them to cool in the fridge.

2. Grab a small bowl and put this stuff in it: the cannabis coconut oil, dill, Dijon, pepper, cayenne, and ground mustard seed. Mix that all together then set the bowl aside.

3. Grab a large bowl and put the walnuts, chick'n, celery, and mashed chick peas in there.

4. Use the contents of the small bowl as a dressing and enjoy!

_____

Gloucester's Space Cake!

Here's what you'll need:

7 tablespoons Cannabis Coconut Oil
3 cups of almonds
½ cup of raw, organic powdered macca
1 cup of pitted dates, soaked for 15 mins in warm water
1 cup of raw, organic powdered cacao
2 tablespoons of chia seeds
1 ½ cups of shredded coconut
½ cup of agave nectar
7 tablespoons of peanut butter

1. Ok, grab a blender or coffee grinder and turn those almonds into a powder.

2. Take your almond powder and mix it with the macca, cacao and 1 cup of the shredded coconut.

3. Now add in the chia seeds, agave nectar, cannabis coconut oil, and peanut butter, and mix it into a dough!

4. Roll the dough out into balls and cover them with the remaining shredded coconut.

5. You can store these bad boys in the freezer until you're ready to get your buzz on!

_____

Aaron's Spicy Hummus
Makes 1 ½ cups (350ml)

1/2 cup of cannabis olive oil
1 belightful habañero chile
2 tablespoons of raw tahini
1 cup of canned chickpeas, rinse and drain those puppies!
The juice from 1 lemon
2 large, minced garlic cloves

1. If you wear contact lenses, pop them out right now before you even start, or brave burning eyes later on tonight.

2. Turn on your broiler!

3. Cut your habanero pepper lengthwise, then pull out and discard the seeds and stems. Pop the sides in a baking dish and let that sit in the broiler until the skin starts to blacken. This should take 10 minutes or so.

4. Take that pepper and pop it in a cool bowl, let it sit there for 15 minutes to cool down. Once it's cool, rub off the skin and mince up its flesh!

5. Now, grab a food processor. Toss everything in there and pulse until you have beautiful smooth hummus!

Othello's Quinoa Tabbouleh
Serves 4

Here's what you'll need:
2 cups (500ml) of water
1/3 cup of cannabis oil
1 cup of rinsed and drained quinoa
1 medium, finely chopped cucumber
3 medium, finely chopped tomatoes
1 cup of scallions, finely chopped
1 ½ cup of fresh, chopped parsley
1/4 cup of pine nuts
1/2 cup of lemon juice
2 tablespoons of fresh mint, finely chopped
Salt to taste

1. Ok, first we're going to boil that water in a medium saucepan. Once it's boiling, add the quinoa, cover it up, and reduce the heat to a simmer. Let that roll for 15 minutes. Once done, set it aside to cool.

2. Meanwhile, in a large bowl, mix the scallions, cucumber, tomatoes and parsley. Then toss in the mint, pine nuts, olive oil and lemon juice.

3. Add the quinoa and mix it all together. Then drizzle on the Cannabis Olive oil!

4. Serve and buzz!

Petruchio's Vegan Fudge

Here's what you'll need:
6 tablespoons of vegan margarine
3 1/2 cups of powdered sugar
1/2 cup of cocoa powder
1 teaspoon of vanilla extract
1/4 cup of plain soymilk
1 cup of chopped walnuts
1/8 oz (30g) of ground, seeds and stems removed

1. Alright, toss together all the ingredients, except the weed and nuts, in a saucepan and let her cook on medium heat for 15 minutes or so, stirring every so often.

2. Now turn off the stove, add your weed and nuts, and mix it well.

3. Finally, pour that bad boy into a baking tray lined with wax paper, and let her cool for an hour.

4. Welcome to the world of magical herby fudge goodness!

___

Pedant's Pecan Pie

Here's what you'll need:

Cake:

1 cup of pecans
1 cup of dates
1 teaspoon of vanilla extract
2 tablespoons of cacao powder

Caramel:

3/4 cup of dates
1 teaspoon of vanilla extract
Cinnamon and nutmeg, to taste
2 tablespoons of Cannabis Coconut Oil, melted
over LOW heat
Water, as needed

Let's top that puppy off with:

Nutmeg
Cinnamon
Pecans

And here we go!

1. Use a food processor to turn those pecans into crumbs

2. Add the rest of the cake ingredients and process until it's combined into a paste

3. Press into a 6 inch springform pan, and leave a little concave so that the caramel doesn't leak over the sides when you pour it later.

4. Leave that puppy in the fridge overnight!

5. Good morning, now it's time for the caramel! Blend all your caramel ingredients and add water if necessary.

6. Pour that delicious caramel over your cake.

7. Now, top that puppy off with the nutmeg, cinnamon and pecans.

8. Eat and get buzzed!

_____

Marcellus' Mango Cheesecake

Here's what you'll need:

Crust
1 ⅓ cups of heaping raw almonds
1 cup of medjool dates
½ cup of of dried coconut
½ teaspoon of vanilla extract
A teaspoon of salt

Filling
4 small mangos
2 limes, zested and juiced
2 heaping cups of cashew kernels (soak those puppies overnight, and drain them)
12 tablespoons of Cannabis Coconut Oil
12 tablespoons of maple syrup
½ cup of coconut cream
¼ cup of fresh mint
2 tsp vanilla extract

And here we go!

1. Grab a food processor and pulse the crust ingredients for about a minute, until it's all mixed and crumbly!

2. Spread the crumbs out in a 10" springform pan, and press them down to form the crust.

3. Now use your food processor to make the filling! Blend together the mangos, vanilla, mint, coconut cream, agave, Cannabis Coconut Oil, cashews, lime juice and lime zest.

4. Pour the filling over the crust and pop that baby in the fridge for an hour.

5. After an hour, pour the maple syrup on top, then pop her back in for another two hours.

6. Enjoy some lovely lovely cheesecake and feel the buzz!

King Lear's Loko Cake!

3/4 cup of Cannabis Vegetable Oil
1 teaspoon of vanilla extract
2 teaspoons of baking soda
1/3 cup of unsweetened cocoa powder
2 tablespoons of white vinegar
2 cups of sugar
3 cups of flour
1 teaspoon of salt

And here we go!

Cake:

1. Ok, let's preheat that oven to 325°F (160°C)

2. Now, combine the salt, baking soda, cocoa powder, sugar and flour in a glass pan. Then, using a knuckle, make three "nests" in mixture where you can pour liquids without them mixing together.

3. In one nest place the vinegar, in the next place the cannabis vegetable oil, and in the third nest place the vanilla.

4. Now drown that whole bad boy with 2 cups of water and whisk it all together! It's ok if this part takes some time.

5. Pop that pan in the oven and let it bake for 50 minutes, using the knife test to check that it's cooked.
Frosting:

Some hot coffee
1 tablespoons of vegan butter
1 tablespoon cannabis coconut oil or vegetable oil
2 cups of powdered sugar
2 tablespoons unsweetened cocoa powder

1. Start out by mixing everything except the coffee, using a pastry cutter or knife may be helpful here.

2. Add the coffee little by little and mix well until you arrive at the right consistency.

3. Get baked on cake!

Brutus' Thunder Balls!

Here's what you'll need:

1 1/2 cups of vegan granola
1/3 cup of vegan chocolate chips
1/2 cup of vegan rice crisps
1/2 cup of peanut butter
1/4 cup of vegan hot coco powder
1/4 cup of agave nectar
2 tablespoons of Cannabis Coconut Oil
1/4 cup of almond extract
3 tablespoons of vanilla extract
1 teaspoon of flax seeds
2 tablespoons of peanuts
3 tablespoons of almond milk

And here we go!

1. Alright, let's grab the peanut butter, Cannabis Coconut Oil, vanilla extract, and almond extract and fold them together in a large bowl. Once they're good and mixed we'll add in the peanuts and flax seeds.

2. Once mixed, transfer the mixture to a pan and cook for 10 minutes over low heat, let it get all good and melty.

3. Once it's melty, add in the hot cocoa powder, agave nectar and almond milk. Let this cook together for another 10 minutes, then turn off the heat to let it cool for a minute or two (until it stops steaming)

4. Pour the granola and rice crisps into that large bowl you used earlier, then pour the peanut mixture over it. Mix it well with clean hands.

5. Roll your mixture into balls and set them onto wax paper.

6. Use the microwave to melt down your chocolate chips, then drizzle the molten chocolate over your peanut buttery balls.

7. Place your balls in the fridge for 30 minutes, then eat them!

_____

Cassio's Stuffed Jalapeños

Yield: 10

Here's what you'll need:

10 beautiful jalapeño peppers
2 tablespoons of Cannabis Olive Oil
1/4 cup of chopped green onions, use only the white parts
2 minced cloves of garlic
3/4 cup of peanut butter

And here we go!

1. Go on and preheat that oven to 350°F (180°C)

2. Ok, now cut the tops of the jalapenos and set them aside. Rinse out the insides of the peppers and remove all the seeds you can.

3. Set the jalapenos on a baking pan lined with foil.

3. Put some Cannabis Olive Oil in a pan and heat it up, then toss in all the ingredients, except the jalapenos.

4. After a few minutes you should have a nice peanut-buttery sauce going in that pan. Pour the sauce into and over the jalapenos, then cover them up with their own tops from earlier. You can use toothpicks to hold them in place if you'd like.

5. Bake the whole thing for 20 minutes and serve warm!

Oswald's Chocolate Chip Cookies

Yield: 24 Cookies

Here's what you'll need:
1 cup of vegan chocolate chips
1/2 cup of Cannabis Coconut Oil
1/4 cup of almond milk
1 cup of light brown sugar
2 cups of flour
1 tablespoon of vanilla extract
1 teaspoon of baking soda
1 teaspoon of baking powder
1/2 teaspoon of salt

And here we go!

1. First, let's preheat that oven to 300°F (150°C)

2. Now, in one bowl blend together the Cannabis Coconut Oil and brown sugar. Once they're good and blended add the vanilla and almond milk.

3. Next, get a separate bowl and use it to mix the salt, baking powder, baking soda and flour. Once those ingredients are mixed together you can mix in the wet ingredients from the other bowl.

4. Now mix in your chocolate chips

5. Roll the mixture out into balls and pop them on a greased baking sheet

6. Bake those bad boys for 10 minutes
7. Once these guys are done baking, you can take them out to cool, eat and tart being baked yourself!

_____

Silvius Space Cookies

Here's what you'll need:

1/2 cup of vegan, black chocolate chips
1/4 cup of almond milk
1/2 cup of shredded coconut
1/2 cup of chopped hazelnuts
1 cup of flour
1/3 cup of sugar
1/2 teaspoon of baking powder
1/2 teaspoon of potato starch
1 cup of uncooked oats
1/2 teaspoon of vanilla extract
A pinch of salt
1/2 cup of Cannabis Coconut Oil

And here we go!

1. Let's preheat that oven to 325°F (160 ° C)

2. Get the salt, oats, flour, and baking powder and mix it all together in a large bowl.

3. In a separate bowl, mix together the vanilla, Cannabis Coconut Oil, sugar, almond milk, and potato starch, then pour half of this mixture into the first bowl.

4. Mix the first bowl again until you have a paste, then add the rest of the contents of the separate bowl and mix again.

5. Now add the coconut, chocolate chips, and hazelnuts and mix them in as well.

6. Roll the mix into balls and back them on a greased baking sheet for 15 minutes.

7. After 15 minutes, remove them from the oven to cool. Once they've cooled off a bit, you can eat your way to heaven!

Made in the USA
San Bernardino, CA
28 November 2016